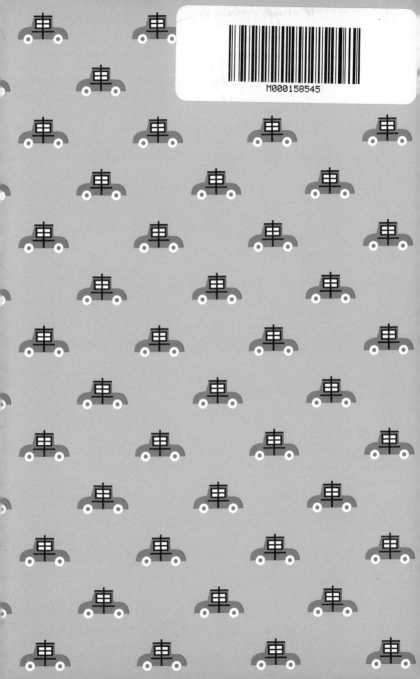

TRAVEL

Chineasy®

TRAVEL

by SHAOLAN 曉嵐
with illustrations by NOMA BAR

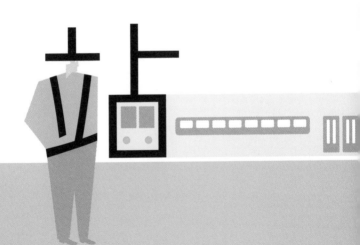

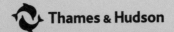
Thames & Hudson

CONTENTS

CHAPTER FIVE: TRANSPORT

CHAPTER SIX: READING SIGNS

CHAPTER SEVEN: REFERENCE

WHAT IS CHINEASY?

Chineasy's goal is to allow people to learn to read Chinese easily by recognizing characters through simple illustrations. The magical power of the Chineasy method is that, by learning one small set of building blocks, learners can build many new characters and phrases. Master a few sets of building blocks, and your learning can be accelerated to a whole new level.

With very little effort, you can quickly learn to read Chinese characters and phrases, and gain a deeper understanding of the historical and cultural references that have influenced the vocabulary. Even though there are tens of thousands of Chinese characters, only around 1,000 are actually necessary to comprehend basic Chinese literature, and to begin to delve into Chinese culture and art.

The Chinese language is traditionally taught through a series of between approximately 180 and 215 radicals. These radicals are then used to form the characters of the Chinese language. *Chineasy Travel* has broken down this collection of characters into their most basic and recurring forms.

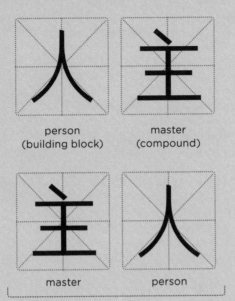

person
(building block)

master
(compound)

master

person

host (phrase)

Building blocks

One building block, or a specific compound form of the building block, can be combined with one or more other characters to make a compound character. Two or more independent characters can be placed next to one another to make phrases.

In compounds, a whole new character is created; in phrases, the placement of characters next to one another gives a new meaning to the collection of characters. The principle of building blocks is what makes Chineasy so easy!

Chinese script

Chinese characters have evolved throughout history, owing to changes of political regime, geographic expansion and the need to address social progress. There are five major historical Chinese writing styles: 'oracle-bone script' 甲骨文 (c.1400 BCE); 'bronze script' 金文 (c.1600–700 BCE); 'seal script' 篆書/篆书 (c.220 BCE); 'clerical script' 隸書/隶书 (c.200 BCE) and 'regular script' 楷書/楷书 (often called 'standard script'; c.200 BCE).

Each writing style has its own distinct features. Oracle-bone script is a set of characters etched on to animal bones or pieces of turtle shell that were then used for divination. Despite its pictorial nature, it developed into a fully functional and mature writing system. Bronze script refers literally to 'text on metals', as these inscriptions were largely found on ritual bronzes such as bells and cauldrons. The development of seal script witnessed the removal of curved or lengthy strokes; Chinese characters written in this style became roughly square in shape. By the time of the introduction of regular script, strokes had become smoother and straighter.

In modern Chinese, regular script is most commonly used in writing and printing, while the earlier writing styles are used as calligraphic art forms.

The evolution of the character for 'sun/day'

| oracle bone | seal script | clerical script | regular script | modern Chinese |

How to use this book

This book teaches both traditional and simplified Chinese, which share a great number of characters. Unless otherwise noted, when the characters differ, the traditional form is given first. Simplified Chinese was adopted in mainland China after the establishment of the People's Republic of China. Traditional Chinese is still used in Taiwan and Hong Kong.

Each character in this book is introduced in its Chinese form, followed by its English translation and then its pinyin (the approximate sound of the character; see page 90). Each building block and compound character (explained on pages 6-7) has a short introduction that teaches you some fun historical and cultural facts as you are learning the language. Also included are unillustrated words and phrases that will help to expand your vocabulary.

At the end of the book there are handy guides to reading, writing and speaking Chinese, plus an index that lists every character and phrase and gives its pinyin. The pronunciation used in this book corresponds to Mandarin only, which is the most widely used Chinese dialect and counts over 960 million native speakers (out of a total of over 1.2 billion Chinese speakers).

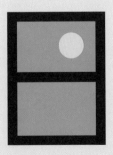

你好 hello (nǐ hǎo)

To say 'hello' in Chinese, we use 你好 (nǐ hǎo). 你 is 'you', and 好 means 'good', so we greet one another with 'you good'!

CHAPTER ONE
THE BASICS

YES AND NO
NUMBERS
MONEY
THE CALENDAR

YES AND NO

好 good/yes (hǎo)

This character is a combination of 'woman' and 'son'.
In ancient China, a woman was required to bear a son
in order to continue her husband's line. This character
can also mean 'yes' or 'OK'.

女 female/woman (nǚ)

This character traditionally
depicted a woman kneeling
showing obedience. See page 80.

子 son (zǐ)

The earliest form of this character
meant 'baby'. It has been extended
to mean 'son'. See page 35.

不 no (bù)

According to statistics, this is the fourth most frequently used character in the Chinese language. In addition to the literal meaning 'no', 不 is essential when you are expressing something negative, in much the same way that the prefixes 'un-', 'im-', 'il-' or 'dis-' are used in English.

When this character appears in a phrase, its pronunciation varies, depending on the character that follows.

NUMBERS

几 how many (jǐ)

This building block looks similar to the symbol for pi (π). Interestingly, its meaning has something to do with maths, too; it means 'how many'. This is the simplified form of the character; the traditional form is 幾.

几 is a very useful question-word. For example, 幾天/几天？(jǐ tiān?) means 'how many days?' and 幾點/几点？(jǐ diān?) means 'what time?'.

 **one** (yī)

The character for 'one' is a simple horizontal line. It comprises a single stroke, known as the heng stroke.

 two (èr)

The character for 'two' is as easy as the number one! You just add a slightly longer horizontal line below 一 (one).

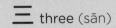 **three** (sān)

The character for 'three' continues the simple pattern of 'one' and 'two' by adding a third stroke, thus 三. 'Three' often indicates 'many'.

四 **four** (sì)

The number four is considered unlucky because it sounds very similar to 'death' 死 (sǐ).

 five (wǔ)

This number is associated with the five elements (see page 40) and the Emperor of China.

六 six (liù)

Originally, this character was a pictograph of a hut, but now 六 is used exclusively to mean 'six' – a lucky number in China, especially in business.

七 seven (qī)

Seven symbolizes 'togetherness', and is auspicious for relationships. In traditional Chinese religions, 49 (7 x 7) is the number of days a deceased person's spirit will remain among the living.

八 eight (bā)

In the Mandarin and Cantonese dialects, the number eight sounds very similar to prosperity' and 'fortune' respectively, which makes it a very lucky number throughout the Chinese-speaking world.

九 nine (jiǔ)

The number nine is also considered auspicious because it's associated with the Chinese Emperor (and with dragons!).

十 ten (shí)

In oracle-bone inscriptions (an early form of Chinese writing; see page 8), 'ten' was represented by a simple vertical line or sometimes a vertical line with a dot in the middle, which was itself a reference to an ancient way of indicating 'ten' by tying a knot in a rope.

Counting from 11 to 99

For the numbers 11 to 19, we use the number 十 (ten) plus whichever number follows it. For example:

11 = 10 (十) + 1 (一) = 十一

12 = 10 (十) + 2 (二) = 十二

And so on; therefore, 19 is 十九.

For the numbers 20, 30, 40 ... to 90, it's also quite straightforward to count numbers by 10s:

20 = 2 (二) × 10 (十) = 二十

30 = 3 (三) × 10 (十) = 三十

The other numbers up to 99 require some simple mathematics. For example:

22 = 2 (二) × 10 (十) + 2 (二) = 二十二

45 = 4 (四) × 10 (十) + 5 (五) = 四十五

MONEY

The official currency of China is the renminbi and its basic unit is the yuan, the name by which the currency is most widely known. One yuan is subdivided into 10 jiao, and 1 jiao into 10 fen (the smallest denomination).

百 hundred (bǎi)

This character looks like 'one' (一) on top of 'white' 白 (bǎi). The earliest form of the character depicted an ancient container with a horizontal symbol at its top to indicate the amount of material inside. It has come to mean 'hundred'.

千 thousand (qiān)

The ancient usage of this character is very different from its modern usage; it used to indicate a man walking endlessly. Its modern meaning is 'thousand'. It might help to imagine a man walking for a thousand miles to get to his destination.

元 dollar (yuán)

In oracle-bone inscriptions, this character depicted a man kneeling down. The two horizontal lines at the top (二) represent the man's head, while the bottom part (儿) represents kneeling. The initial meaning of the character was 'head' or the 'beginning' of something, since the head was emphasized in the original script. Today it has been extended to mean 'dollar'.

one   hundred   dollar

一百元 one hundred dollars (yī bǎi yuán)

THE CALENDAR

月 moon/month
(yuè)

In addition to meaning 'moon', the character 月 also means 'month'. Traditional Chinese calendar months are measured in lunar cycles. The dates of many Asian holidays and festivals are still determined by the traditional calendar. However, almost everyone in Asia today, including the Chinese, uses the Gregorian calendar for official business.

Writing the month

When stating the months in Chinese, you just need to add the character 月 (moon) after the relevant number between 1 and 12, as you can see in the two examples below.

January

one   moon

一月 January
(yī yuè)

August

eight   moon

八月 August
(bā yuè)

日 sun/day (rì)

Originally, the character for 日 was a circle with a dot in the middle, so it looked more like a 'sun' than the modern character. Eventually, the dot in the centre became the horizontal line we see in the middle today, and the circle became a rectangle. This character also means 'day', because we think that the day starts when the sun comes up and finishes when the sun goes down.

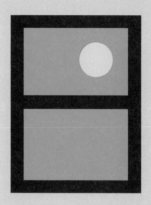

Days of the month

The days of the month are written in a similar way to the months of the year: you just need to add the character 日 (sun/day) after the relevant number between 1 and 31.

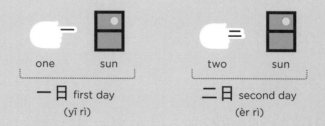

| one | sun | | two | sun |

一 日 first day
(yī rì)

二 日 second day
(èr rì)

Writing the date

In English, we may say either 'January 2nd' or '2nd January', but in Chinese, the word order for phrases relating to time always progresses from 'big' to 'small'. So, you start with the year, then the month, then the day and finally the time.

January 2

一月 January
(yī yuè)

二日 second day
(èr rì)

August 12

八月 August
(bā yuè)

十二日 twelfth day
(shí èr rì)

CHAPTER TWO
WHERE IN CHINA

PROVINCES AND CITIES
DESCRIBING THE LANDSCAPE

PROVINCES AND CITIES

China is one of the world's largest countries, both by area and population size. Over 1.4 billion people live in its provinces, regions and municipalities, from remote mountain communities to densely populated urban areas.

京 capital (jīng)

What's the place where all the tall buildings and prominent government officials are situated? It's the capital. 京 is the character for 'capital', and originally it depicted a grand building sited on high ground.

吉林 Jilin

北京 Beijing

山西 Shanxi

山東 Shandong

南京 Nanjing

上海 Shanghai

四川 Sichuan

長江 Yangtze River

north   capital

Beijing

北京 Beijing (běi jīng)

north + capital = Beijing

Beijing means 'north/northern capital'. This name was first used during the Ming dynasty (1368–1644), but it became widely accepted only in 1949, at the founding of the People's Republic of China. The city has a population of over 21 million.

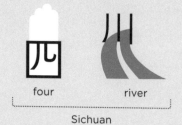

four   river

Sichuan

四川 Sichuan (sì chuān)

four + river = Sichuan

There are various theories about the name 四川: it can refer to 'four' 四 main 'rivers' 川, but it can also mean where 'four plains' meet (in addition to 'river', 川 means 'plain'). The population of the province is 82 million.

above   sea

Shanghai

上海 Shanghai (shàng hǎi)

above + sea = Shanghai

Shanghai – meaning 'above the sea' – is the biggest and busiest city in China. It began as a small agricultural village and developed only during the late Qing dynasty (1644–1912). Since then, it has become the most populous city in the world, with over 24 million inhabitants – that's more people than live in the whole of Taiwan!

mountain   east

Shangdong

山東 Shandong (shān dōng)

mountain + east = Shandong

Shandong province takes its name from its location, east of the Taihang Mountains (太行山; tài háng shān). It has a population of 97 million. The simplified form is 山东.

DESCRIBING THE LANDSCAPE

The names of provinces, cities, towns and villages in Chinese-speaking countries often have their roots in surrounding geography. Here are some basic characters that describe the landscape.

水 water (shuǐ)

This character originally had a winding line in the centre, showing how water flows, and dots on both sides, representing drops of water.

川 river (chuān)

There are a few characters in Chinese that have remained relatively unchanged since ancient times. This character is one such example; it's always been written as three slightly wavy lines. You can think of its left-hand stroke as a bend in the river!

海 sea (hǎi)

This character is a combination of the compound form of 'water' 氵 and 'every' 每 (měi). You can also see 'mother' 母 in it. Every drop of water in our rivers and streams eventually makes its way to the sea, just as children return to their mothers.

山 mountain (shān)

In oracle-bone inscriptions, this character depicted three mountain peaks. These peaks are still evident in the three vertical lines in the present form of the character.

木 tree (mù)

The building block for 'tree' represents a tree trunk with hanging branches. When this character is used as an adjective, it refers to a wooden texture.

林 woods (lín)

Two trees together make a wood, which is greater than a single tree.

森 forest (sēn)

Three trees make a forest, which is greater than a tree or a wood. When used as an adjective, this character means 'dense', just like a thick cluster of trees.

CHAPTER THREE
CHINESE CULTURE

DYNASTIES AND EMPERORS
RELIGION
YIN AND YANG
CHINESE MEDICINE
FENG SHUI
CHINESE FESTIVALS
THE CHINESE ZODIAC

2100 BCE —	
	Xia Dynasty (c.2100– c.1600 BCE)
1600 BCE —	
	Shang Dynasty (c.1600– c.1050 BCE)
1050 BCE —	
	Zhou Dynasty (c.1050– c.256 BCE)
221 BCE —	Qin Dynasty
206 BCE —	(221–206 BCE)
	Han Dynasty (206 BCE–220CE)
220 —	
	Six Dynasties Period (220–589)
581 —	Sui Dynasty (581–618)
618 —	
	Tang Dynasty (618–906)
907 —	Five Dynasties Period
960 —	(907–960)
	Song Dynasty (960–1279)
1279 —	Yuan Dynasty
1368 —	(1279–1368)
	Ming Dynasty (1368–1644)
1644 —	
	Qing Dynasty (1644–1912)
1912 —	Republic Period
1949 —	(1912–1949)
Present —	People's Republic of China (1949–)

DYNASTIES AND EMPERORS

China was ruled by dynasties for much of its recorded history, from 2100 BCE until the establishment of the Republic of China in 1912. The People's Republic of China was established by the Communist Party in 1949.

The Xia Dynasty was the first according to Chinese tradition and the earliest known examples of Chinese writing, oracle bone script, date from this period. This script is the precursor to Chinese characters as we recognize them today.

The first emperor of a unified China was Qin Shi Huang (259–210 BCE), who founded the Qin Dynasty. He is remembered for the Qin Walls, early components of the Great Wall of China, and for the vast terracotta army buried with him upon his death. Discovered in 1974, his grand mausoleum was filled with over 8,000 sculptures of soldiers, chariots and horses, which were presumably intended to protect him during the afterlife.

sky/heaven   son

emperor

天子 emperor (tiān zǐ)

heaven + son = the son of heaven
This is the imperial title of Chinese monarchs, founded on the
ancient philosophical concept of the Mandate of Heaven.

天 sky (tiān)

When you put a line on top of 'big' 大,
it means 'sky' or 'heaven'. Traditionally,
the line represented the spiritual level
above man and earth. This character
can also mean 'day'.

子 son (zǐ)

This character is based on an oracle-bone
inscription depicting a baby, complete with
an oversized head and a few wispy hairs.

RELIGION

Many Chinese people find that their lives are governed tightly by Buddhism, Taoism and Confucianism, even if they are not religious or they belong to a different faith. Together, these three doctrines provide guidance on how society should function and what its virtues should be.

Developed by Confucius (551–479 BCE), Confucianism is an ethical and philosophical system that guides people's behaviour in society. It came to prominence after Emperor Wu of the Han dynasty (206 BCE–220 CE) adopted it as the state ideology. The principles of Confucianism played a crucial role in the formation of the values, culture and mentality of the Chinese people. Confucianism also provided a strict social hierarchy, which was a convenient tool for those in power. In Confucianism, everyone fits within various social classifications and ranks. A person's place in this hierarchy governs both their behaviour and how they are judged by the community.

Founded upon the teachings of the Buddha, and introduced into China some 2,000 years ago, Buddhism has developed into the most important religion in the Chinese-speaking world and has become one of the largest global religions. It has had three main areas of influence: literature, art and ideology. The important Buddhist texts are the Lotus Sutra, Nīlakantha Dhāranī and Diamond Sutra.

Taoism dates back to the 3rd century BCE. Its ancient texts are the I-Ching and Tao-Te Ching. Its development over the centuries has sometimes been besmirched by charlatans peddling alchemy, life elixirs and talismans. Taoism as a religion, distinct from Taoism as a philosophy, has a rich palette of sacrament and ritual, with temples, monasteries, priests and ceremonies, and gods and goddesses of all kinds for believers to worship.

佛 Buddha (fó)

This character is a combination of the compound form of 'person' 亻 and 'not' 弗 (fú). The composition of the character expresses well one of the basic concepts of Buddhism: it is not about the person (亻), it's a way of life and gives purpose to life. When we do 'not' (弗) have to consider a person's desires, we will be able to achieve enlightenment, and we will become the 'awakened one', like Buddha.

YIN AND YANG

Yin and Yang as a philosophical framework can explain all disciplines of knowledge in Chinese culture.

Yin has slow, soft, pliable, diluted, cold, wet, cloudy, dark, shady, secret and passive qualities; it is aligned with water, earth, the moon, femininity, night-time and a negative electrical charge.

Yang has fast, hard, solid, concentrated, hot, dry and aggressive qualities; it is aligned with fire, sky, the sun, masculinity, daytime and a positive electrical charge.

However, Yin and Yang are not static absolutes, and nothing is entirely Yin or completely Yang.

陰 Yin (yīn)

Yin means 'feminine', 'female', 'cloudy', 'dark', 'shady', 'secret' or, in the context of electricity, 'negative'. This character, 陰, is a combination of 'hill' 阝 (fù), 'cloud' 云 and 'now' 今 (jīn). So, when clouds gather around the top of a hill, it is dark. The simplified form is 阴.

In philosophy, Yin and Yang represent truth and falsehood, meaning that nothing is absolutely true or totally false. For thousands of years, Chinese people have understood that there is no clear-cut boundary between yes and no, right and wrong, or good and evil.

陽 Yang (yáng)

This character is a combination of 'hill' 阝, 'sun' 日 or 'sunrise' 且, and 勿 (wù). In the traditional form, 昜 means 'bright', having originally depicted 'sun' 日 with 'rays coming down' 勿. The simplified form is 阳.

CHINESE MEDICINE

Traditional Chinese medicine has been part of everyday life in East Asia for thousands of years and includes acupuncture (針灸/针灸; zhēn jiǔ), herbal medicine and therapies connected to exercise, diet and massage.

| water | fire | wood | earth | metal |

The five elements

There are five elements in tranditional Chinese medicine, water (水; shuǐ), fire (火; huǒ), wood (木; mù), earth (土; tǔ) and metal (金; jīn), and each person is born with a composition of all five. It is this unique blend of elements that forms the basis of your personality and constitution. The 'qi' (vital force) of the five elements waxes and wanes in daily and seasonal cycles. The theory behind Chinese medicine is that a person becomes sick owing to an imbalance of these elements.

Internal organs are each represented by one of the five elements and this dictates the appropriate treatments for certain medical conditions. For example, the liver and gallbladder are associated with wood, the heart and small intestine with fire, the stomach with earth, the lungs and skin with metal, and the kidneys and bladder with water.

The perfect balance

In traditional Chinese medicine, one is healthy only when Yin and Yang are in balance. Without the warming properties of Yang, an excess of Yin may lead to poor circulation, cold limbs, pale skin and low energy. An excess of Yang, however, may result in headaches, nosebleeds, sore eyes and throat, a reddening of the skin, irritability and manic behaviour. Using the principle of Yin and Yang, Chinese medicine is prescribed to compensate for any imbalance, with the aim of restoring a perfect equilibrium.

疒 to indicate illness (nè)

The building block 疒 doesn't exist as a stand-alone character. It indicates illness when you see it combined with other characters. The shape of 疒 originally resembled a sick person sweating in bed.

Describing symptoms

疼 ache (téng)

痛 pain (tòng)

牙痛 toothache (yá tòng; tooth + pain)

頭痛／头痛 headache (tóu tòng; head + pain)

FENG SHUI

Sometimes known as the 'art of placement', Feng Shui is a practical way of understanding and appreciating the harmony between people and their environment.

Feng is 'wind' and Shui is 'water'; together they make 風水/风水 (fēng shuǐ). It is commonly associated with interior design (it offers useful guidance on lighting, energy preservation, ventilation and comfort), but for thousands of years the Chinese have used Feng Shui principles in urban planning, agriculture and architecture. In ancient times, a ruler would consult Feng Shui masters before deciding the location of a new capital, settlements and fortresses. They had to consider the supply of food and water, the effects of heat and cold, the likelihood of floods and storms, the position of roads to connect to the rest of the kingdom, and any military advantage in defending their people.

Before the invention of the magnetic compass, Feng Shui masters were experts in astronomy; they studied the alignment of the stars in order to decide where to build homes. Recent research has indicated that over six thousand years ago the dwellings of the ancient Bampo civilization were sited so that they gained maximum heat from the sun. Since then, Feng Shui has developed into a complex theory influencing the daily lives of billions of people. There have been numerous schools of thought over the years. While they all have followed the same general principles, inevitably a number of them have adapted contradictory practices, some more extreme than others.

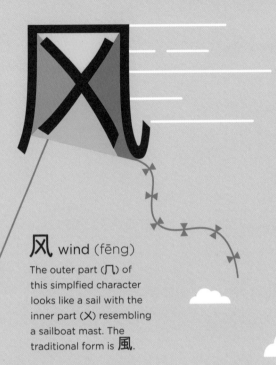

风 wind (fēng)

The outer part (几) of this simplfied character looks like a sail with the inner part (乂) resembling a sailboat mast. The traditional form is 風.

水 water (shuǐ)

CHINESE FESTIVALS

Chinese New Year

Chinese New Year (春節/春节; chūn jié) marks the turn of the traditional lunar calendar, with fifteen days of celebrations that start each year on the new moon. The first day of the festival therefore varies from year to year in the Gregorian Calendar and is usually a date between late January and late February. A major holiday in Asia, it is celebrated by Chinese-speakers around the world.

New Year festivities traditionally include a 'reunion dinner' with family on New Year's Eve, red decorations (red is considered auspicious and is the traditional colour of the festival), firecrackers, street processions and the exchange of red envelopes containing money to pass on luck and good wishes.

The fifteenth and final day of New Year festivities is celebrated with the Lantern Festival (元宵節/元宵节; yuán xiāo jié). People light and float beautifully decorated lanterns, visit lantern fairs, guess riddles written on lanterns and watch dances in the streets. Each Chinese New Year is attributed to an animal of the Chinese Zodiac according to a twelve-year cycle (see page 48). Each animal is thought to bring its own characteristics to those born within that year.

福 blessing (fú)

This character means 'good fortune' or 'blessing'. It is commonly written on red paper during Chinese New Year.

Qixi: Chinese Valentine's Day

Qixi (七夕; qī xī) is a traditional festival celebrating the annual meeting of separated lovers in Chinese mythology. It's also called 'Double Seventh' because it always falls on the 7th day of the 7th month (七月七日; qī yuè qī rì) of the traditional lunar calendar. Depending on the year, this means it usually falls on a date in July or August. The myth concerns the forbidden love between Cowherd and Weaver Girl. Banished to opposite sides of the river, they can only reunite for a single day each year by crossing a bridge of magpies.

Dragon Boat Festival

The Dragon Boat Festival (龍舟節/龙舟节; lóng zhōu jié), falls on the 5th day of the 5th month (五月五日; wǔ yuè wǔ rì) of the traditional lunar calendar. Depending on the year, this means it usually falls on a date in May or June. It is commonly thought to have started following the suicide of the famed poet and statesman Qu Yuan, who took his life by drowning in the river. The legend goes that men on the shore rushed to the nearest boats to try to save him, but were too late. Although the origin of the festival is tragic, the modern festival is one of celebration.

THE CHINESE ZODIAC

For thousands of years, the twelve-part zodiac has influenced daily life in China on many levels. The earliest literature that mentions the zodiac dates back to the Qin dynasty (*c.*220 BCE), with a small difference being that the Dragon is a Bug in that version.

豬
pig
zhū

狗
dog
gǒu

鸡
chicken
jī

猴
monkey
hóu

羊
sheep
yáng

馬
horse
mǎ

The twelve animals became the labelling system for the calendar (years and months) and the time (in ancient China, every two hours represented one unit in a day).

Theories have been developed to predict one's personality, fortune and major life decisions on the basis of the characteristics attributed to each animal of the zodiac.

鼠

鼠
rat
shǔ

牛
cow
niú

虎
tiger
hǔ

虎

兔
rabbit
tù

兔

龙
dragon
lóng

龙

蛇
snake
shé

蛇

The dragon is probably the most important and symbolic animal in Chinese history. Chinese people call themselves 'the descendants of the dragon'.

Millions of Chinese people firmly believe the happiness of their marriage is determined by the 'perfect match' of a couple's zodiac. For example, a Dragon matches a Rat, Monkey and Chicken auspiciously, but matches a Cow, Rabbit, Dog or another Dragon adversely. The belief system extends to every kind of human relationship, such as between parents and their children, and among siblings, colleagues and friends. The Chinese also believe that children born into a certain zodiac will have better luck and fortune than others. Having a Dragon boy is the dream of many families, as Dragon babies will supposedly have a prosperous career and good fortune.

鼠 rat (shǔ)

This character is simply the pictograph of a rat. It may be rather a strange image, but imagine a rat wearing a nice top and a pair of trousers with a four-dotted pattern! In Chinese, there is no significant difference between mice and rats, so they share this character.

牛 cow (niú)

The original form of this character meant 'ox' or 'cattle', and depicted the face of an ox with upward-pointing horns. In time, the strokes depicting the horns became a left-falling stroke and a horizontal stroke, and the character came to mean 'cow'.

虎 tiger (hǔ)

虎 is one of the pictographic characters from ancient China. When it is used as an adjective, it means 'brave'. The character 唬, 'to scare' (hǔ), is a combination of 'mouth' and 'tiger'. Imagine how scared you would be to hear a tiger roar in the middle of the night.

兔 rabbit (tù)

In oracle-bone script, the character for 'rabbit' depicted a rabbit on its side. Over time, rabbit features have been added. You can remember the character by thinking that the top part (ク) represents the rabbit's long ears, with its eyes in the middle and its strong back legs at the bottom. And how about that little dot on the right side of the character? It's the rabbit's tail, of course!

龙 dragon (lóng)

This legendary creature has the antlers of a deer, the head of a crocodile, the eyes of a demon, the neck of a snake, the viscera of a tortoise, the claws of a hawk, the palms of a tiger and the ears of a cow. The dragon is believed to have auspicious powers that control rainfall. The traditional form is 龍.

蛇 snake (shé)

The character for 'snake' is a combination of 'bug' 虫 (chóng) and 它 (tā). In ancient scripts, 它 meant 'snake', but the character was later borrowed to represent 'it'. To differentiate between the two, a 'bug' was added next to 它 to show 'snake'.

馬 horse (mǎ)

In the illustration, you can see the horse is on its side, and that's how our ancestors designed this character. The simplified form is 马.

羊 sheep (yáng)

In oracle-bone script, this character depicted a sheep's face with a pair of horns. Over time, the face became the two lower horizontal strokes (the third stroke used to be part of the horns). Today the character represents the goat-antelope subfamily of mammals.

猴 monkey (hóu)

This character is a combination of 'dog', indicating the meaning, and 'lord' 侯 (hóu), indicating the pronunciation.

鸡 chicken (jī)

This is the simplified form of 'chicken'; the traditional form is 雞, which, according to its etymology, depicts a huge bird 鳥 that is tied up and teased (奚) for people's pleasure.

狗 dog (gǒu)

The more commonly used character for 'dog' is a combination of 犭, indicating the meaning, and 'sentence' 句 (jù), indicating the pronunciation.

豬 pig (zhū)

豬 is now commonly used to refer to 'pig', but the ancient character 豕 (shǐ) featured a long snout, a big belly, hooves and a tail. You can still see the original character as a building-block on the left-hand side of 豬.

CHAPTER FOUR
FOOD AND DRINK

EATING AND DRINKING
RICE AND NOODLES
MEAT DISHES
TEA AND WINE

EATING AND DRINKING

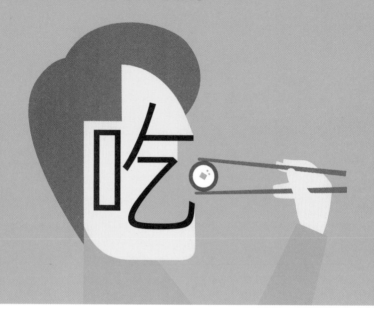

吃 to eat (chī)

This is probably the most important character in Chinese history! When people greet you in China, instead of asking, 'How have you been?', they often enquire, 'Have you eaten?'

Street food is part of daily life for most Chinese, and indeed across the whole of Asia: millions of people have their breakfast, lunch and even dinner at street-food stalls every day.

small + to eat = street food/snack 小吃 (xiǎo chī)

喝 to drink (hē)

This character is a combination of 'mouth' 口, indicating the meaning, and 'a shouting noise' 曷 (hé), indicating the pronunciation. One way to remember the meaning of the character is to think that when we shout loudly, we become very thirsty and so we then need to drink.

to drink + water = drink water 喝水 (hē shuǐ)

米 rice (mǐ)

In oracle-bone inscriptions, this character depicted uncooked grains of rice on a wooden rack. In seal inscriptions, the rack became a cross (十), and the rice was indicated by four dots.

米 usually refers to husked, uncooked rice. The character 飯 (fàn; simplified form: 饭) means 'cooked rice'. To most Chinese people, a bowl of cooked rice turns any dish into a hearty meal. It's no wonder that China produces and consumes more rice than any other country.

面 noodle (miàn)

This is the simplified form of 'noodle'; the traditional form is 麵, which is a combination of 'wheat' 麥 (mài), indicating the meaning, and 'face' 面 (miàn), indicating the pronunciation. The simplified form of 'noodle', 面, was chosen as a replacement for the traditional form, 麵, because the characters are pronounced identically.

If we put 'noodle' 面 and 'powder' 粉 together, we make the phrase for 'flour': 麵粉/面粉 (miàn fěn). This phrase is easy to remember because most noodles are made from flour.

MEAT DISHES

肉 meat (ròu)

The original form of this character looked like a thick piece of meat with exposed veins. In its modern form, the veins have been transformed to look like one 'person' 人 standing on top of another, and the component 冂 represents the outline of the meat.

The character 肉 is also very useful when we refer to meat, poultry and fish. We build phrases in this simple way: 'animal name' + 'meat'. Opposite are some examples of what you might see on a menu in China.

cow + meat = beef 牛肉 (niú ròu)

pig + meat = pork 豬肉/猪肉 (zhū ròu)

sheep + meat = lamb 羊肉 (yáng ròu)

chicken + meat = chicken (poultry) 雞肉/鸡肉 (jī ròu)

fish + meat = fish 魚肉/鱼肉 (yú ròu)

TEA AND WINE

茶 tea (chá)

I always imagine this character as a person 人
wandering through a garden of tea trees 木,
picking the tips of the tea leaves 艹.

酒 wine (jiǔ)

This character is a combination of 'three dots of water' 氵
and 'wine vessel' 酉. It is actually a general noun indicating
an alcoholic beverage, such as 'wine', 'spirit' or 'liquor'.

In a Chinese restaurant the waiter may ask if you want
酒水 (jiǔ shuǐ; wine + water).

wine + water = alcoholic/non-alcoholic drink 酒水 (jiǔ shuǐ)

Why you should never refuse a toast

The culture of toasting is very important in China. Traditionally, the host toasts their guests to honour them, and it's considered rude if you don't drink. If you're going to propose a toast, make sure you toast everyone who outranks you. You can do two or three at once if you want to avoid a headache the next morning! Stand up, which puts you in an inferior position to those who are seated, and drain your cup. The others may remain seated and drink or do the same as you. If clinking glasses, make sure your glass is lower than the other person's. This shows respect. The original toast was 'gānbēi', which means 'drying the cup'. If you didn't down your drink, this was seen as disrespectful. Now people may use 'suíyì' ('as you wish').

CHAPTER FIVE
TRANSPORT

CAR, BUS AND TRAM
TRAIN
BOAT AND AEROPLANE

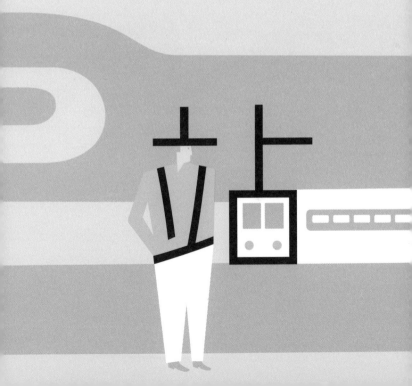

CAR, BUS AND TRAM

車 car (chē)

This character represents a wooden cart and means 'vehicle'. In ancient China, carts were mainly used as part of the battle force during war; the more carts you had, the stronger your army. Gradually, carts of this type came to be used for transporting goods and people, too.

A more common definition for 車 is 'car'. Sometimes the phrase 車子 (chē zi) is used instead. While the character 車 can be used on its own, the addition of the suffix 子 emphasizes that you are referring to the modern vehicle. The simplified form of the character is 车.

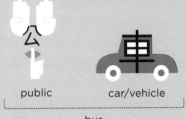

public   car/vehicle

bus

公車 bus (gōng chē)

public + vehicle = bus

The characters 'public' 公 (gōng) and 'vehicle' 車 together
`mean 'bus'. Another common way to express 'bus' is
公交車/公交车 (gōng jiāo chē). 交 (jiāo) means
'to exchange', 'to intersect'.

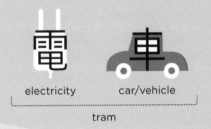

electricity   car/vehicle

tram

電車 tram (diàn chē)

electricity + vehicle = tram

Electric cars are becoming increasingly popular these days,
but actually the earliest form of transport powered by
electricity was the tram; that's why 'electricity' 電 plus 'vehicle'
車 means 'tram'. The longer phrase 電動汽車/电动汽车
(diàn dòng qì chē), which translates literally as 'electricity move
automobile', is used to refer to 'electric car'.

TRAIN

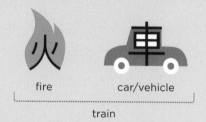

fire   car/vehicle

train

火車 train (huǒ chē)

fire + vehicle = train

Trains were originally powered by steam and fire,
so that's why 'fire' 火 plus 'vehicle' 車 means 'train'.
The simplified form is 火车.

站 stand/station (zhàn)

This character is phono-semantic (or pictophonetic): 'to stand'
立 (lì) indicates the meaning, while 'to occupy' 占 (zhàn)
indicates the pronunciation. When it is used as a noun,
the character commonly means 'stand' or 'station'.

| fire | car/vehicle | station |

train station

火車站 train station (huǒ chē zhàn)

train + station = train station.

The simplified form is 火车站.

| public | car/vehicle | station |

bus station

公車站 bus station (gōng chē zhàn)

bus + station = bus station.

The simplified form is 公车站.

BOAT AND AEROPLANE

舟 boat (zhōu)

This character depicts the shape of an ancient Chinese wooden vessel, which looked similar to a punt. 舟 is quite an archaic way of expressing 'boat'. Today we tend to use the compound character 船 (chuán), which is a combination of 舟, 'how many'/'small table' 几 and 'mouth' 口.

If you see 舟 in a compound character, you know it means something to do with boats or ships. For example, 'sampan' 舢 (shān) — a flat-bottomed wooden boat — is a combination of 'boat' 舟 and 'mountain' 山.

flying   machine

aeroplane

飞机 aeroplane (fēi jī)

flying + machine = aeroplane

What comes to your mind when you think of a 'flying machine'? An aeroplane, of course! See below for an explanation of the component characters. This is the simplified form, the traditonal form is 飛機.

飞 to fly (fēi)

Originally, this character depicted a bird flapping its wings and flying upwards. Its meaning has been extended to indicate 'to fly'. When it is used as an adjective it means 'flying'. The traditional form is 飛.

机 machine (jī)

This character is a combination of 'tree' 木 and 'how many' 几. The traditional form is 機.

大夫

CHAPTER SIX
READING SIGNS

POINTS OF THE COMPASS
LEFT AND RIGHT
UP AND DOWN
ENTRANCE AND EXIT
PUBLIC AND PRIVATE
FEMALE AND MALE
POLICE AND DOCTOR

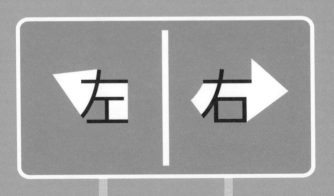

POINTS OF THE COMPASS

The cardinal directions always appear in the order 東西南北/东西南北, when mentioned together in Chinese.

東 east (dōng)

When we see the 'sun' 日 coming up between the 'trees' 木, we know we're looking 'east' 東. The simplified form of the character is 东.

西 west (xī)

In oracle-bone script, this character represented a nest. In seal script, a bird was added next to it, to indicate that birds retire to their nests. Later the character came to mean 'west', since after a day spent flying around, tired birds head home when the sun sets in the west. This character looks a bit like a cowboy in the Wild West.

南 south (nán)

Originally, this character was a pictograph of a percussion instrument. This meaning has been lost for a long time, and now the character only means 'south'. One strong association with the south are penguins in Antarctica.

北 north (běi)

In oracle-bone script, this character depicted two people standing back to back, and it meant 'back'; it has now evolved to mean 'north'. One way to visualize the character is as two people, with their backs to each other standing out in the cold north wind.

LEFT AND RIGHT

左 left (zuǒ)

In oracle-bone inscriptions, this character depicted a left hand. Later, its meaning became simply 'left'; however, the trace of 'left hand' can still be seen in the modern form of the character, in the component ナ.

右 right (yòu)

The character for 'right' has an ancient origin similar to that of the character for 'left', 左; originally, the character 右 depicted a right hand. The component 'mouth' 口 was added later at the bottom, so remember this character by thinking that a right-handed person uses their 'right' 右 hand when eating.

UP AND DOWN

上 up/above (shàng)

In oracle-bone script, the character for 'up' looked very much like the character for 'two' (二); the bottom line indicated the earth's surface, while the upper line indicated anything above the earth. It wasn't until the bronze script, when a vertical line was added, that this character came to resemble its modern form.

Besides representing such prepositions as 'up', 'above' or 'on top of' and the adjective 'upper', 上 can indicate such verbs as 'to ascend', 'to go up' or 'to climb'.

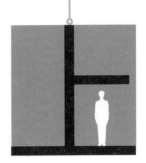

丅 down/below (xià)

The original form of the character for 'down' also resembled the character for 'two' (二); however, the upper horizontal line was longer than the lower line. The evolution of the form of this character was very similar to that of the character 上 as well.

In much the same way that 上 has various meanings, 丅 has several usages besides 'down', including 'below', 'lower', 'to descend', 'to go down' and 'to get off'.

ENTRANCE AND EXIT

to enter	mouth

entrance

入口 entrance (rù kǒu)

to enter + mouth = entrance

This simple phrase contains the building blocks 'to enter' 入 (rù) and 'mouth' 口 (kǒu). In this context, 口 means 'entrance', just like the mouth is an entrance into the body, and the character 入 refers to the act of entering.

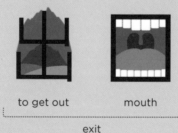

to get out	mouth

exit

出口 exit (chū kǒu)

to get out + mouth = exit

A 'mouth' 口 that tells you where 'to get out' 出 (chū) means 'exit'.

公 public (gōng)

The ancient form of the character depicted an earthen jar with a curved handle on top. Later, it came to mean 'public', 'fair' and 'common'.

私 private (sī)

The character for 'private' 私 (sī) shares the same component 厶 as 公.

女 female/woman (nǚ)

In oracle-bone inscriptions, this character depicted a woman squatting down with her arms folded across her body. This was a sign of submission, as women were regarded as the possessions of men. In Chineasy you see it represented as an independent, witty and feminine lady. She is her own person. In the context of family relationships, 女 means 'daughter'. When used as an adjective, it means 'female'.

男 male/man (nán)

In oracle-bone inscriptions, this character depicted a man with 'power' or 'strength', 力, in his arm, carrying out work in a 'field' 田 (tián); the two components sat side by side. The character has evolved so that, in its modern form, 力 has relocated under 田 to become 男. When used as an adjective, this character means 'male'.

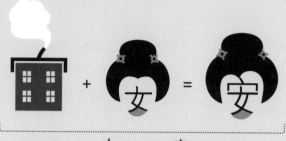

宀 roof + 女 woman = 安 peaceful

public　　peaceful

police

公安 police (China) (gōng ān)

Police combines the characters for public + peaceful
In Taiwan 'police' is 警察 (jǐng chá), which is
police + to observe.

big   man

doctor

大夫 doctor (dài fu)

This phrase has two meanings. When pronounced 'dài + fu', with a neutral and soft tone, it means 'doctor'. When pronounced 'dà + fū', it means 'senior official'. Both are rather archaic. The modern term for 'doctor' is 醫生/医生 (yī shēng).

Other useful signs

機場/机场 airport (jī chǎng)

救護車/救护车 ambulance (jiù hù chē)

銀行/银行 bank (yín háng)

醫院/医院 hospital (yī yuàn)

酒店 hotel (jiǔ diàn) or 飯店/饭店 (fàn diàn)

飯館/饭馆 restaurant (fàn guǎn)
or 餐廳/餐厅 (cān tīng)

超市 supermarket (chāo shì)

地鐵/地铁 metro/subway (dì tiě)

CHAPTER SEVEN
REFERENCE

READING CHINESE
WRITING CHINESE
SPEAKING CHINESE
INDEX OF CHARACTERS AND PHRASES

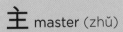 master (zhǔ)

This character originally meant 'wick' or 'torch'
but today means 'master', 'owner' or 'host'.

READING CHINESE

Chinese can be read either horizontally or vertically. In fact, you can read from left to right, right to left, or top to bottom. The only direction you won't find is bottom to top.

Today the most common style is from left to right, in the same way that English, French, Spanish and German are read.

In ancient literature or on road signs in China, you will sometimes see phrases written from right to left. This can seem odd in literature that mixes both English and Chinese.

If you are trying to read vertically (if you are reading scrolls, for example), then you would read from right to left, starting with the first vertical line on the right from top to bottom, and then moving towards the left edge of the scroll.

Spacing

How can you tell if you are reading a character (字) or a phrase (詞/词)? A character, whether it's a building block or a compound, fits within one square.

When you see two people squeezed together in a single square, you know it's a character – for example, the simplified character 'to follow' 从.

A phrase, on the other hand, is spaced across two or more squares. That means, if you see two or more characters spread across two or more squares, then you know it's a phrase – for example, 'everyone' 人人.

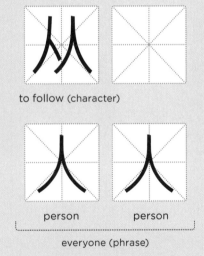

to follow (character)

person　　　　person

everyone (phrase)

The beauty of the Chineasy method is that you can construct many new 'words' by combining existing characters. Chinese characters rarely appear alone; it is often only in the context of a phrase that the meaning of a character becomes clear.

WRITING CHINESE

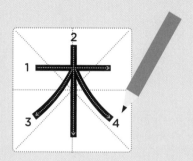

Everyone who studies Chinese has to go through this exercise when they learn how to write. Each character has to be drawn neatly inside a square. You can see that a single tree fits into a square the same size as the squares used for 'two trees' and 'three trees'.

You should see a slight alteration of the shape from the original 'tree': in order to fit two trees side by side in the square, you must make thinner trees. When three trees are stacked together, all the trees are shorter in order to fit into the square. In Chinese, certain building-block characters have an alternate form that appears only when used as part of a compound. These characters are traditionally known as 'piānpáng' 偏旁. On the right, you can see an example of this in the 'person' 人 = 亻 compound form in the compound 'group' 伙.

Even though there are several different spoken Chinese dialects, such as Mandarin or Cantonese, they all share the same written characters; it is only the pronunciation of these characters that will differ from one dialect to another – often completely.

tree

person

two trees = woods

person
(compound form)

three trees = forest

group

SPEAKING CHINESE

To teach Mandarin Chinese to non-native speakers, most teachers use pinyin, the standard phonetic system for transcribing the sound of Chinese characters in the romanized alphabet. Chinese is a tonal language, so the pinyin system uses a series of either numerals or glyphs to represent tone. For instance, the pinyin for 'no' can be written as either bu⁴ or bù. Chineasy uses the glyphs pinyin system. After every English translation, you will see a word in brackets with accents; these act as guides to the pronunciation of the character.

First tone = high-level tone
Second tone = medium rising tone
Third tone = falling rising tone
Fourth tone = falling tone
No accent = brief and soft tone

First tone
high-level tone

Second tone
rising tone

Third tone
falling rising tone

Fourth tone
falling tone

No accent
brief and soft tone

不 no (bù)

Basic grammar

Chinese grammar is easy for a couple of reasons.

First, verbs do not take different tenses. In English, we must distinguish between the tenses. For example: I drive a car (present simple); I am driving a car (present continuous); I have driven a car (present perfect); I drove a car (past simple); I will drive a car (future). In Chinese, we just add the time – today/tomorrow/yesterday/one hour ago, etc. – at the start of the sentence.

Secondly, in Chinese there are no strict rules about gender. In spoken Chinese, 'he', 'she' and 'it' are all pronounced as 'tā'. In written Chinese, there are gender distinctions: 'he' 他 (with a 'person' building block), 'she' 她 (with a 'woman' building block) and 'it' 它. However, many people always use 'he' 他.

Yes/no questions

In Chinese, there are several ways to ask a yes/no question. One common way is to add the question indicator 嗎/吗 (ma) to the end of a sentence.

For example:

你高。 'You are tall.' (nǐ gāo)

你高嗎/你高吗？ 'Are you tall?' (nǐ gāo ma?)

The order of the characters is the same in the two sentences above, but the second sentence ends with the question indicator 嗎/吗, which turns an affirmative sentence into an interrogative one.

INDEX OF CHARACTERS AND PHRASES

山	mountain (shān)	31
九	nine (jiǔ)	16
不	no/not (bù)	13
麵/面	noodle (miàn)	57
北	north (běi)	72
一	one (yī)	15
痛	pain (tòng)	41
人	person (rén)	7, 87
豬	pig (zhū)	46, 51
公安/警察	police (China: gōng ān; Taiwan: jǐng chá)	82
豬肉/猪肉	pork (zhū ròu)	59
私	private (sī)	79
公	public (gōng)	79
七夕	Qixi (festival) (qī xī)	45
兔	rabbit (animal) (tù)	47, 49
鼠	rat (shǔ)	47, 48
飯館/饭馆 or 餐廳/餐厅	restaurant (fàn guǎn or cān tīng)	83
米	rice (uncooked) (mǐ)	56
飯/饭	rice (cooked) (fàn)	56
右	right (yòu)	75
川	river (chuān)	30
海	sea (hǎi)	30
七	seven (qī)	16
山東/山东	Shandong (shān dōng)	27, 29
上海	Shanghai (shàng hǎi)	27, 29
她	she (tā)	91
羊	sheep (yáng)	46, 50
四川	Sichuan (sì chuān)	27, 28
六	six (liù)	16
天	sky (tiān)	35
蛇	snake (shé)	47, 50
子	son (zǐ)	12, 35

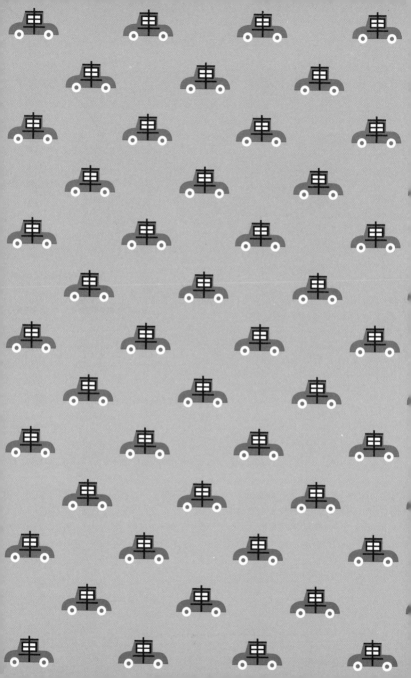